GHOST ARSON

Poems by Barton Smock

Kung Fu Treachery Press

Rancho Cucamunga, CA

Copyright (c) Barton Smock, 2018
First Edition 1 3 5 7 9 10 8 6 4 2
ISBN: 978-1-946642-86-8
LCCN: 2018964278

Design, edits and layout: John T. Keehan, Jr.
Cover image: John E. Epic
Author photos: Aidan Smock

Kung Fu Treachery Press would like to thank The Black Dragon Poetry Society, The Nu Prophets of P/O/E/T/I/C Dischord, The Fellowship of N-Finite Jest, The Osage Arts Community, Stubborn Mule Press, Jeanette Powers and John P. Waterman.

CONTENTS

Periapt / 1

Vein / 2

Scansion / 3

Dying Boy When Did Fate Begin / 4

Cleaning the Body Small and Boy / 5

A Gun Goes off in a Dream I Don't Have Anymore / 6

Elevation Songs / 8

Moonhood / 9

Starlit / 10

Wrist Musics / 11

Gameshow Fatalities / 12

Houndlings / 14

Untitled / 16

Returning / 17

Wrist Musics / 18

Stopping to Pray / 19

Gestural Transportation / 20

Concern / 22

Nymph / 23

Bee Pain / 24

Snow / 25

Rare Disorders in the Very Young / 26

Boy Musics / 27

Tube Feeding / 28

Thorn / 29

Removal Musics / 30

Muscle Musics / 31

Dust Musics / 32

Core Musics / 33

The Upper Body of the Minotaur Lost Everything / 34

I Still Bring Snow / 36

Being Alone Went by so Fast / 37

How I Want You to Remember My Sister / 38

Rabbit Horns / 39

Sailboat / 42

Prayers for Small / 43

By Horse I Mean / 44

Motive / 45

Ohio Musics / 46

On Peacelessness / 47

Having a Disabled Child / 48

Response Musics / 49

A Prayer for the Tall Mother
    Whose Cigarettes Void Brevity / 50

Ghost Arson / 51

Predictive Text / 52

Mooon / 53

Asking / 54

Rarefactions / 55

Waker / 56

Materials / 57

Materials / 58

Materials / 59

Insomniacs for the Health of Your Ghost / 60

Supply / 61

Kite / 62

For Genevieve, Mary Ann, Noah, Aidan, and Timothy. Apparitions, all.

Periapt

I saw nothing fantastic.

an angel
freezing to death
in a somersault. a mirror

coming out of its skin. emptiness

the size of a pea
no pea

empty

Vein

in the blue church of my father's thirst

I wear it

(hunger)

like an eye-patch, and emerge

starless

from the uncooked blood
of my shadow

Scansion

it feels wrong to pray in an ambulance

hear god / all the time

Dying Boy When Did Fate Begin

there was a radio somewhere in the basement and we
knew this because it would click on long enough for us
to cover our feet and question our savior's second go
at amnesia. if I wasn't there, I was probably trying out
my father's fastball with a grip he called the ribs of my
neighbor's dog. not long from this I was holding a baby
and said what a vague hiatus. also in this order I may
have said you look like a ghost and then not my finger
but a finger does snap into place when I smoke.

Cleaning the Body Small and Boy

the brain a nude
in the remoteness of god

A Gun Goes off in a Dream I Don't Have Anymore

the root of the animal's insomnia is not man but the fear of personification.

-

when my uncle was a baby, he tried to put something in his mouth but couldn't do it.

-

grief is the herd my sadness trails.

-

my mother returns every year to the same spot as if it's a microwave.

-

before he goes back to providing the radio play-by-play for an obscure sporting event, father lifts up his shirt to show me the wire jesus wore.

-

while smoking a cigar in the shadow of a nervous minotaur, my father wrote the book on moral isolation. in it, he predicted there would be a television show about hoarders and that it would turn god into a sign from god. my mother read the book cover to cover during her fourth and fastest delivery. if there were edits, she kept them to herself and put his name beside hers on seasonally produced slim volumes of absolute shyness.

-

death takes its place at the head of the table to tell the only story it knows to plates of untouched food.

-

trespassing, I approach two dimming flashlights set upright in cemetery mud that in your recollection are the horns of an empty beast.

-

as spotless as the dog left it, the baby's room has come to mean today. above a different dog, people ask us what we're having. we do our jigsaw of darkness. clone the ape that created god's boredom.

-

I find the boy's name on a list in another boy's diary. a gun goes off in a dream I don't have anymore.

Elevation Songs

there's no great detail to go into. her baby in a medicine
cup, our small priest

making us feel poor in the bathroom we don't use...

-

a face from the world's flattest mirror

Moonhood

as if waiting
for you
to hallucinate

it is there

the sea

-

eating secrets in a dream

is the owl
with hands

-

I think we buried
darkness
wrong

Starlit

after staring all day at a birthmark, father asks can he
wear my glasses. done growing, sister breaks her nose.
shadows mother from birdbeak to mudmask.

Wrist Musics

grief
is a red-haired jesus
whose barber
puts a dollhouse
mirror
on my mother's
tongue

blood
is water's
favorite
child

at the baptism
some agree
that my father
knows
his milk, others

that any creature
on four legs
has one
ghost
knows how
to swim

Gameshow Fatalities

it is a midwestern vaccination to declare that eventually
everyone you know will exist. I have been leaving clues. one
model airplane per claustrophobe. sleep works but only if
you picture god as a toddler studying a map. chickens don't
dream. tornado takes up for glacier.

-

dear grief, was it ever just us? you, the hesitant psychic of
sorrow. and me. there to lower magic into the rabbit-death

of a cornered orphan.

-

on a normal day, there is a before and an after and a bit of
mystery to the meal-obsessed. father says we're fasting in
a world of spirits. my shyness is a chair sent from a distant
church. my belly button is how the marksmen touch me.
our house is chosen by strangers for its elbow room. the
baby is a ghost and will be until it starts teething. brother
has a pencil and sister her longhand's impossible loss.
mother is checking the dogs for ticks by the light of a bulb
from a hospital lamp. grief makes a cat because it's what
grief can do with its eyes closed. anything unplugged is able
to remain a secret. every mouth is a nightmare nightmares
notice.

narrative is dead. is not a boy with a long illness.

-

see my brother in some who are not. my son as my son.
a tooth as the mirror of milk and milk as having hair god
longs to comb.

see one of my children worrying less about suicide and
more about where it should happen. see: tub. see: easier
for a mother to clean.

Houndlings

as hunger's sole worry is that revenge has no one, I do not
reply when the boy gets an erection so painful that he says
he can see me sleeping in his past. what does your stomach
know of mine? to believe in beauty is to let blood do all the
work.

-

it's midnight and our mail carrier is trying to recall aloud a
proverb in a language she doesn't know. her hound, barefoot
and dressmaker, has two names. she wants to smoke but can't
bring herself to imagine god's forgotten thumb. her tv is on
and I watch it as if dreaming was always a sin.

-

it skips our father like a language the meal she pulls from her
tinfoil purse and god he stops at the roof of my mouth and
brother short of beheading an egg...

(fluency

our only comet

-

as written, the word

why

looks a thing forgiven mid-bite. a chicken scratch left
behind the ear of a boy by an angel erring on the side
of pink. a puzzle piece blocking the airway of a god
with a tail. a worm suspended in the grey afterlife of a
swimmer

once the weigher of nothing's limb.

-

grief the star of my overlong nostalgia
& owl the mouth I put on god

(in dream the embedded curfew

-

god is just a patient creature that swallowed a lonely. did
you love him? as an infant blowing kisses to a bruise. a
mother born to look seen.

a father has these dogs:

death, sound, & ageism.

Untitled

sister played outside with a broken arm and the wind turned her into a constellation. - Allie Gilles

a piece of ice
in my mouth
I'm kissing
a screen door
in Ohio

eternity
is a doll
reading
a menu, memorizing
a license plate

and doll
the first

eating disorder
in space

Returning

my angel is a scarecrow in a sleeping bag. heaven a
movie theater in spain. she walks that way because she is
trying to step on her blood. the boy at the gate is lost and
must choose either frankenstein's childhood or a more
diverse nostalgia. orphans on earth smell like bread.

Wrist Musics

this crow
with its black
worm
knows your father
feels loss
in the neck

Stopping to Pray

how angelic
the nervousness
of insects
offering acne
to god

/ to glacier, crow is not
yet a thing

Gestural Transportation

in the idea, god creates only those creatures already
identified by the man he can't shake.

-

I am quiet but nobody listens.

I am loneliest when it's not allowed.

-

after a child drowns in a child, the church bathroom is
scrubbed in full view of the elderly.

-

while thunder remains god's most solemn prank, the
moon is the bottom of a prop tree. there are egg shells
on
the floor of heaven.

-

the bread crumbs were eaten not by birds but by a
starving boy with a lost voice who'd wandered from his
home in a delirium brought on by a toothache. also,
Hansel & Gretel were two rich kids who killed someone's
mother.

-

god goes from wall to wall unaware he is god disguised as a
graffiti artist.

renderings of my son on a ventilator adorn the moving city.

-

in flight, a wasp carries something it's not. forgiveness works alone.

-

I have never seen an attractive god.

Concern

I pass my son in the hallway

instar
and throe

our unpracticed sleep
our elbows

he learns this way
of my mother, her father, the nothing

time does

Nymph

yesterday I sent to my mother grief as an attachment

-

it continues to matter
the spell
your god
is under

-

(what began as nostalgia is now

Bee Pain

all of your mother's paintings have two names. father
with cigarette or jesus

meet ghost.

-

four pounds / of my birth / were missing

Snow

say even god / would leave / this church

to step on the bones of a star

Rare Disorders in the Very Young

in a nightmare

(praying over
his father
to highlight
the size
of the first
computer)

he disproves

god

(son) who breathes

for a snake
made of milk

Boy Musics

we're counting cigarettes on the roof of a closed sex shop
in Ohio when I tell you my father is gay. it's too late for
crow and all the deer have been hit. you have just read
me three poems by your dead sister, the third of which
she called dead sister. a vacuum is running below us.
you ask me if I've ever wanted to see her handwriting. it's
nothing like yours but maybe one day.

Tube Feeding

the boy who in the middle of performing a handstand
finds god just as she's creating the oceans after being
overtaken by a herd of ghosts

Thorn

the dream
bread
of insect, horn

of dust

Removal Musics

flicking cigarettes from the highest car of a stopped ferris
wheel, we sing at how sex is the centaur's trap door. you

are telling rain
not to look. there are jobs

no one gets. abacus / mascara / there are words

responsible
for your mother's
face. it is more pregnant

to bury
a footprint.

Muscle Musics

a tadpole
in my mouth
I pin
with my knees
my smallest
brother
our first
kiss
on the cross
of the startled
mime

Dust Musics

the treehouse oven, the breadlit

moon- so what

he don't remember
right or left
which hand
shot
his brother, how many

fish
per nightmare

Core Musics

i.

a long-legged owl
its blood
gone to heaven
her shadow
drops everything

ii.

I don't eat where I eat

iii.

ear-shaped mirrors. junkyard deer

The Upper Body of the Minotaur
Lost Everything

mother prays for odd things. like passwords. and that
there be one day a mirror she can warn.

-

my father was born with six fingers on his right hand
and seven on his left. he was not fond of either hand
until later in life when the grandchildren asked him at
different times during their visits if he had been tortured.

-

my brother says it's part of his condition that he can only
explain himself from the waist down. before I can play
doctor, he remembers he has a story he wants me to
write. in the opening scene a young man is blowing dust
from a human skull made of plastic because it's all the
narrator can afford.

-

your sister is the only person on record to have been
born without a gift. I was told this in confidence by an
angel masquerading as a small animal the size of which
escapes me.

-

excuse my friend his earlier joy in saying who do I
have to fuck to get fucked around here. at age 19 a man
exploded beside my friend and my friend went quiet and
later to his grave thinking his own bomb malfunctioned.

-

I know it's early but I need you to make sure there are no
bugs on your father before he goes to work.

I Still Bring Snow

I think mom's new dog must have the bones of a kite. I have
a lover, now. a he, a beekeeper. a she if she saddens in the
nearness. a nothing, a dowry. ghost china. spacesuits for
stillborns. under this blanket, a puppet reads to a doll about
light. under that, the shape of what goes blind in a poem. I
miss you. plural. I don't wash my forehead. I still bring snow.

Being Alone Went By So Fast

we have in my city a museum just like this. I, too, am
private and have lost an unabsorbed child. I am,

inventory, very motherly.

this one-man radio show about a father looking for his
mouth. this tornado.

my first owl was a bee-loving tick. my first milk
was jigsaw

milk. being alone went by so fast.

How I Want You to Remember My Sister

in a puppet show
about washing
my son's
feet, or waving down

the ice cream truck
with her bible, or

as farewell

to nothing's
church
of neither

Rabbit Horns

a plastic doll with a human right hand distracts us from
the parrot's empty cage. we have been writing in unison
instead of eating. our poverty is so advanced it keeps a
fake diary and a real diary but hides them in the same
spot.

-

I saw my youngest brother born. I saw his mouth. I
thought he'd ripped.

-

the dark, the ocean. I have two reasons to believe god
has not stopped creating. my anger has gone the way of
the milkman. his doomed child with her piece of chalk.

-

it is childish how much time she thinks I have to touch
everything in the store. I am slapped so hard I am sure
the mirror's memory is for show.

-

my father holds a cigarette above his head in a hotel
shower. at home, my mother puts a clean shirt on the
bed and jumps from her death.

-

I am secretly happy that you've taken an egg for each day
of your life to a doll so doll can sleep. as your mother, I
often follow a black ball of yarn into the lake of how you
remember.

-

a male mime bites into a bar of soap...

-

her father is just as she imagines-

a man not making siren sounds pulled over by the man
who is.

-

you will know the hoof of satan's chosen deer by the way
it glows when any female announces from the seat of a
stilled tractor that she is pregnant. you will be the age of
your mother's baby bump, older than your father's knife,
and lit by the grape in god's mouth.

\-

I am in the saddest grocery waiting with my mother for the happiest bike repair to open.

\-

dodgeball, no one sad.

Sailboat

his sister, three years away from leaving social media,
has a boyfriend whose depression is a feminist. darkness
lands again the role of weather. on paper, his cough is
somewhere between cricket and cross.

Prayers for Small

that I be baptized by a vandal whose frostbitten hands...

that I could touch you with what I'm seeing and that a
thing be worth

no words.

By Horse I Mean

dropped from a hand-shaped dream

were three fish the length of my beating...

-

your ghost town anthills

this blank
taxi

seeable

porn

-

by horse I mean
thing without a ghost / that we followed with our hair

Motive

I threw
a couple sticks
and waited
to be kissed
on the arm
while my brother
licked
from his leg
the first insect
to have
amnesia
pretty soon
after that
our sister
bought a car
that had hit
a puppy
the puppy
lived
and god
was hooked

Ohio Musics

a call-in radio show
the listeners
of which
are asked
to describe
loneliness
in their own
words

(sexual

 farness)

to a coal worker
or a clown

On Peacelessness

no jump
scare
this losing
of child
to sheepish
math

Having a Disabled Child

means
it is enough
this morn
that the weak
kneed
angel
of small
hands
dreams
from the disposal
the rabbit's
foot

Response Musics

I thought girlhood the boyhood of grief

childcare, handprints, the failed hearts
of octopi

toy / on a stair / left there / by doll

god (memory)
making its way
through the useless
infant

myself
an impressionist

(because all

my mothers
faint

A Prayer for the Tall Mother
Whose Cigarettes Void Brevity

piano that disappeared
milk
that didn't…

feather in the stomach
of my angel's ghost

Ghost Arson

i.

so happens
that his first
circus
reminds him
of the circus

ii.

any creature
smaller
than a dog
should get back
in the dog

iii.

I lost my hair
or began
to lose
my hair   in a cornfield

Predictive Text

he knows three languages
but hurts me
in one

-

our baby hasn't spoken in years

-

we were left two insomniacs

they are slowly
picking teams

-

satan has no memory of passing through deer

Mooon

moan, fossil. how do my feet look in my mother's belly?
my heart is a pink flame / is my father's / fingernail.
father calls me antler. I don't know this yet. I will be
shot

by many hands.

Asking

can I miss
my body
with yours
our blood
the loneliest
bone

Rarefactions

for Kazim Ali

pain has no spirit, I am never

so sad
that I can't
scrape
the neighbor's
car, probably

you won't
survive, babies

are all
the same, I recite

what sounds
pretty, it seems

less happens
in the winter, to animals

and bread

Waker

mouth pain / in a clean / house

-

the weight
of sister

-

the passwords of worried creatures

a stroller's
body
of work

-

treeless (quiet)

Materials

mothers
while jumping
rope
reminisce
on those
crucifixions
not postponed
by thunder

Materials

eating for the child lost by ghost, you are the second of
three people who know god's middle name. oh how I've
written to avoid reading. to impress death.

a babysitter's tattoo. the bird-sleep of ache.

Materials

she is cooking with the father of an ex-lover a meal for
someone who's just had surgery. god is there but might
as well be listening for thunder. she hopes the dream is
not a big deal.

Insomniacs for the Health of Your Ghost

in one dream, a carousel horse. in another, a stomach.

-

dream is a shortcut

Supply

mother and father
pass
back and forth
a bruise
they call
wristwatch

how long
was I drunk
learning curve

of cocoon

Kite

even
longing
loses
me

Barton Smock lives in Columbus, OH with his wife and four children. He is the author of the chapbook *infant* cinema* (Dink Press, 2016) and editor of *isacoustic** (isacoustic.com)

BLACK DRAGON POETRY SOCIETY

CERTIFIED AND APPROVED